This is a story
about a little dog
with a special gift
who learns about the
magical world of music.

Scherzo's Magical Musical Adventure

Story and Oil Paintings by
Nancy E. Bennett

Whiterabbit Designs

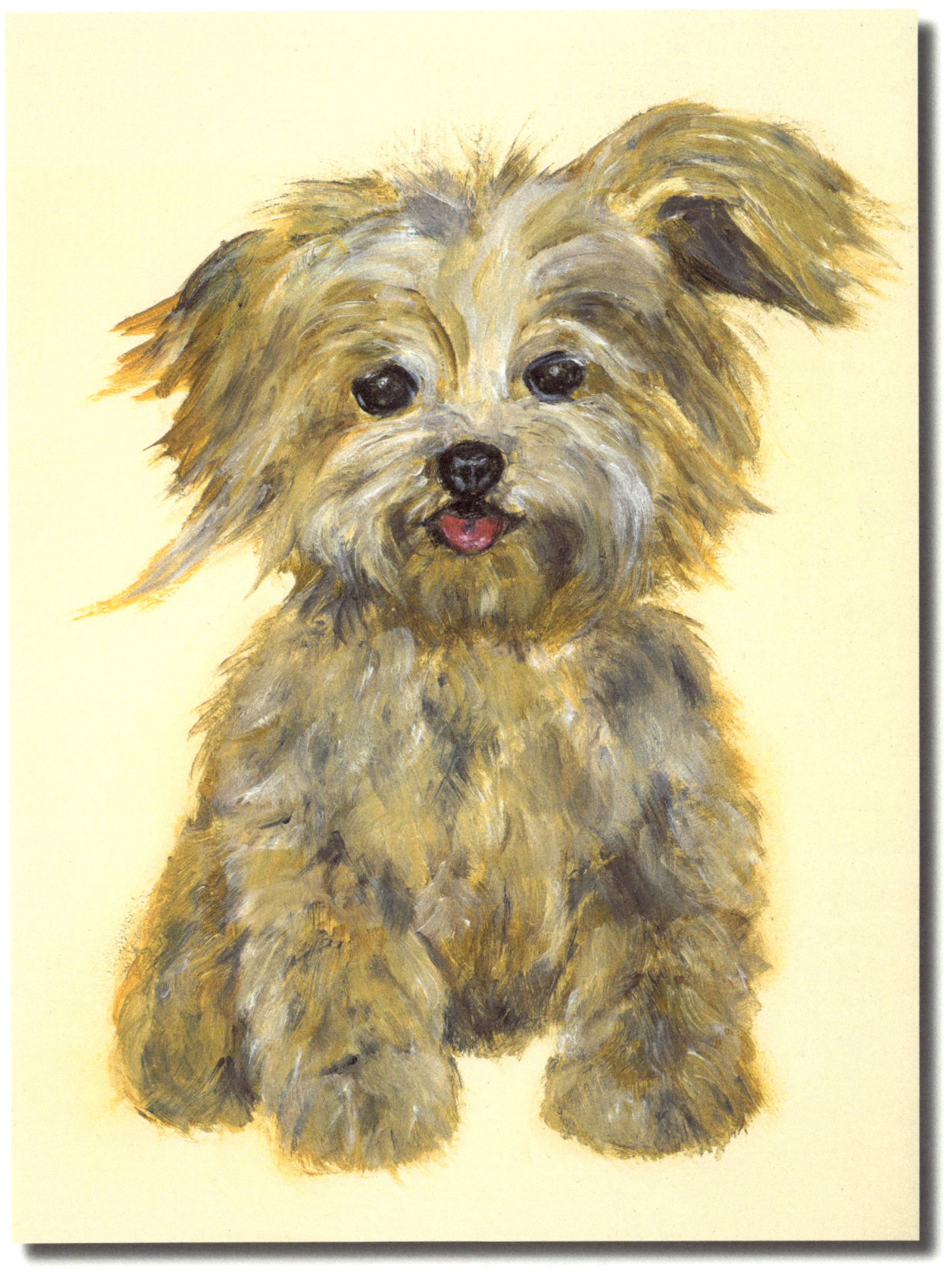

This book is dedicated to the animals
Who are the music of my life

I wish to acknowledge the friends and students who have inspired and supported the writing of this book. It is my sincere desire that it will help to introduce children to musical topics in a unique way, so as to inspire learning and creativity.

I hope the adventure will be 'magical!'

Nancy E. Bennett

Scherzo was a very special dog. He could sing! He was the only one in his family who could. His brothers and sisters used to make fun of him when he sang because he was so different from everyone else.

What they did not know was his singing was a wonderful gift. So Scherzo would go to the meadow where he could sing his heart out much to the delight of the creatures who lived there.

One day a stranger who was passing by heard him singing. It was Professor Guin who stopped to listen from behind a tree. Professor Guin had a music school where singers went to learn to be good musicians as well as good singers.

After hearing Scherzo sing, Professor Guin said, "You have a lovely voice." "Thank you," said Scherzo. "I really love to sing."

"I have a school for singers where you could meet others like yourself. Would you like to visit?" "Oh, yes." "What is your name young sir?" "Scherzo" (scare-tzo), the pup said. "That's a very musical name. Come, let's go. I have much to show you."

So off to the office of Professor Guin they went.

In the Office of Prof. Guin

The Professor had a book with some things
Scherzo would learn.

"In this book," said the Professor, "are words
that tell us about how to sing the music. To go
fast or slow or loud or soft. Let me show you a
few of these words."

And when Scherzo opened the book,
this is what he saw.

Presto

(press toe)

fast, like a busy hummingbird

Legato

(ley ga toe)

smooth and even
like a swan on a lake

Staccato

(sta ca toe)

short little sounds like hopping rabbits

Hop hop hop!

Vivace

(vee va chay)

like a lively,
running horse

Andante

(an don tey)

not too fast and not too slow,
like friends walking nicely together

Largo

(lar go)

slow like elephants
sometimes walk

Piano

(pea an oh)

means softly

(shsss don't wake the puppy)

The sign for this is:

P

or PP, very soft

Forte

(four tey)

loud
like a lion roaring

Sometimes just a sign for this word
is like this:

F

or FF, even louder

"By the way,
your name Scherzo means playful,
like a good joke,
you know, happy music!

"Now a singer needs to 'read' the music
(to name the lines and spaces)

"These lines and spaces have names like the alphabet,
except only A thru G are used."

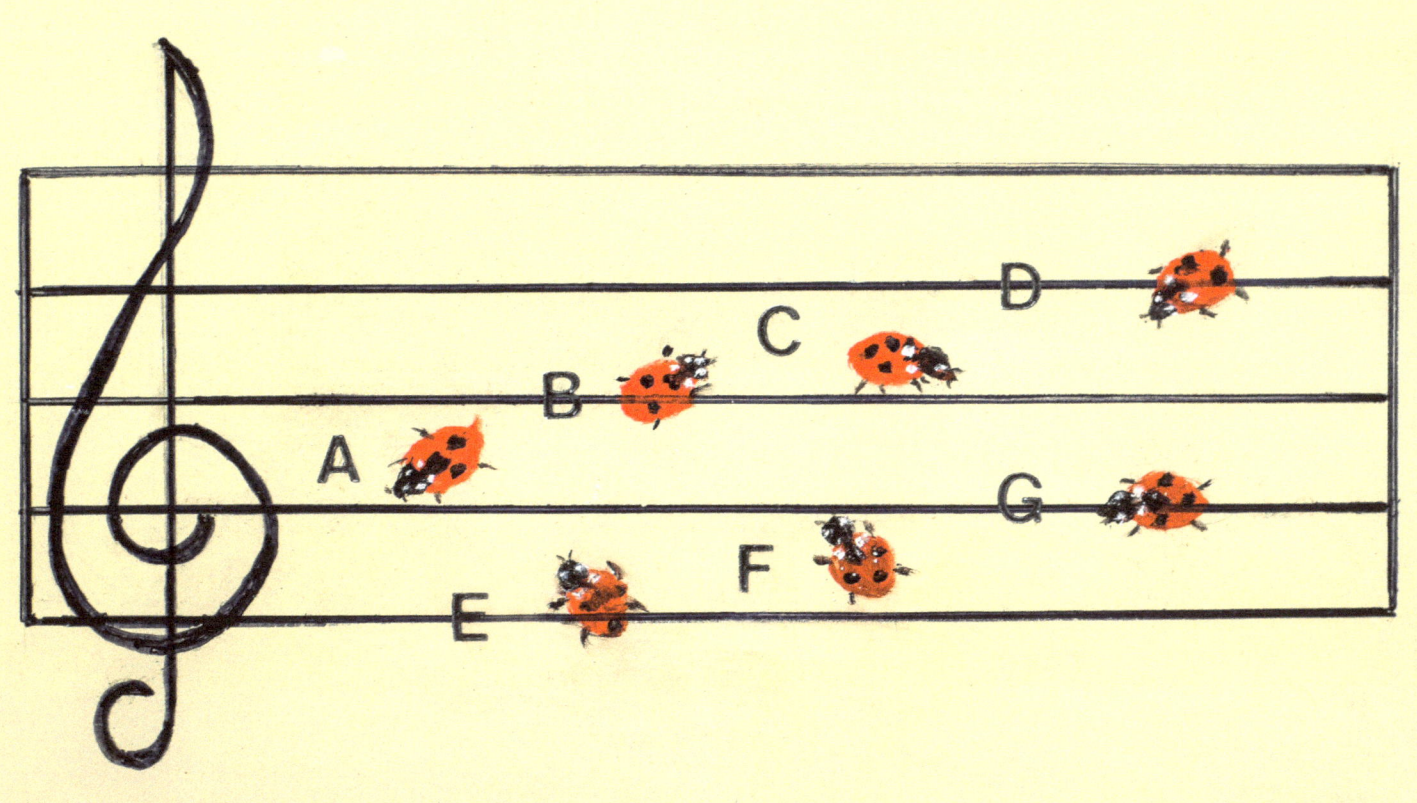

"Did you know that there are different kinds of voices? Some sing high and some sing low."

S A T B

"What kind of a voice do you think I have?" asked Scherzo.

"Well," the Professor said, "we will have to see once you are in class."

"And there are groups of singers you can join.

"Everyone singing together is a chorus,
both high and low voices and some in between.

"This is a good place for you to start.

"My little son is in the chorus."

"Oh," said Scherzo, "that would be magical."

"And there are other groups," said the Professor, "including singing alone."

Solo

a song
for one

Duet

a song for two

Trio

a song for three

Quartet

a song for four

Singers have to look good when singing,
so here are the Sun Sisters
showing how to stand
and how to bow.

Standing nice and tall
hands (leaves) at the side

Thanking
the audience
when you are done
(they loved you!)

When you are finished singing everyone claps and you smile and bow

"Well what do you think?" asked Professor Guin. "If you work really hard, maybe you could sing a solo with the choir one day."

So Scherzo went to school and worked very hard
to be a good singer and musician
and was asked to sing a solo with the chorus:
his dream come true.

He did so well that everyone enjoyed the concert very much.

Some of the chorus members were jealous
because they wanted the solo,
but the lesson here is: if they study hard and practice
they can sing just as well as Scherzo and realize their dream.

and SO CAN YOU !

ABOUT THE AUTHOR

Nancy E. Bennett has been teaching voice for over 40 years to students ranging from children to professionals. She holds an M.A. degree in Voice. As Assistant Professor at California State University and Chaffey College she gave voice lessons, taught music appreciation and music theory, and was music director for the theatre productions. She has been a member of the National Association of Teachers of Singing for 40 years.

As a professional singer, Nancy has appeared as soloist with the Los Angeles Philharmonic under the baton of Zubin Mehta, the Carmel Bach Festival, the Los Angeles Master Chorale and several European tours, in addition to many recitals and productions in the Los Angeles area. She is a self-taught oil painter.

An avid animal lover and supporter, she feels that in writing this book she has combined her three passions—love of singing, teaching, and animals.

Nancy lives in Carmel, California, and gives private voice lessons, leads a community voice class, and teaches voice at Santa Catalina School in Monterey.

Copyright © 2020 Nancy E. Bennett
All rights reserved

Oil paintings by the author

Published by Whiterabbit Designs
Carmel, California

ISBN: 978-0-578-67068-3

This book contains images and text protected under International and Federal Copyright Laws and Treaties. No part of this book may be reproduced or transmitted in any form or by any means whatsoever without express written permission from the author.

Designed and produced by
Ginna and David Gordon
Lucky Valley Press, Jacksonville, Oregon
www.luckyvalleypress.com

Printed in the United States of America on acid-free paper.

www.ingramcontent.com/pod-product-compliance
Lightning Source LLC
Chambersburg PA
CBHW041322290426

44108CB00004B/106